American Battlefields

THE ALAMO

MARCH 6, 1836

Mark Stewart

ENCHANTED LION BOOKS
New York

© 2004 White-Thomson Publishing Limited
and Enchanted Lion Books LLC

Published in the United States of America in 2004 by
Enchanted Lion Books, 115 West 18 Street, New York, NY 10011

Library of Congress Cataloging-in-Publication Data
Stewart, Mark 1960-
The Alamo, February 23-March 6, 1836 / Mark Stewart.
p.cm - (American Battlefields)
Includes index.
ISBN 1-59270-026-8
1. Alamo (San Antonio, Tex)—Siege, 1836—Juvenile literature
I. Title. II. Series.
F390.S8 2004
976.4'03—dc22   2003069609

Created for Enchanted Lion Books by
White-Thomson Publishing Limited
Bridgewater Business Centre
210 High Street
Lewes BN7 2UH

Titles in the series American Battlefields:
The Alamo
Gettysburg
Lexington and Concord
Little Bighorn

Editorial Credits
Editor: Peg Goldstein
Designer: Clare Nicholas, based on a series design by Jamie Asher
Consultant: Steve Mills, Ph.D., Keele University
Proofreader: Alison Cooper
Picture Research: John Klein
Artwork: Peter Bull Studio

Enchanted Lion Books
Editor: Claudia Zoe Bedrick
Production: Millicent Fairhurst

Printed in China by South China Printing Company

Picture credits
Benson Latin American Collection/University of Texas at Austin 11(t);
British Museum/Angelico Chavez History Library 5(t); Center for
American History/University of Texas 14(t), 18; Corbis 7(t), 14(b),
17(b), 27(b), 28(b), 29; Daughters of the Republic of Texas Library
P. O. Box 1401, San Antonio, Texas, 78295-1401 17(b); Friends of
Governor's Mansion title page, 23(t); Institute of Texan Culture at
UTSA 11(b), 27(b); Peter Newark 4, 24(t); San Jacinto Museum 9, 26;
Southwest Museum cover, 22; Texas State Library and Archives
Commission 7(b), 8(t), 8(b), 11(t), 13(t), 15, 19, 20(t), 20(b), 21,
23(b), 24(b), 25;
Witte Museum 5(b), 6.

*Disclaimer: The website addresses (URLs) included in this book were valid at
the time of going to press. However, because of the nature of the Internet, it is
possible that some addresses may have changed, or sites may have changed or
been closed down since publication. While the author, packager, and publisher
regret any inconvenience that this may cause readers, no responsibility for any
such changes can be accepted by either the author, packager, or publisher.*

*Every effort has been made to trace copyright holders. However, the publisher
apologizes for any unintentional omissions and would be pleased in such cases
to add an acknowledgement in any future editions.*

Cover art: Dawn at the Alamo (1905). Courtesy of Southwest Museum.
Title page art: Fall of the Alamo. Courtesy of Friends of Governor's Mansion.

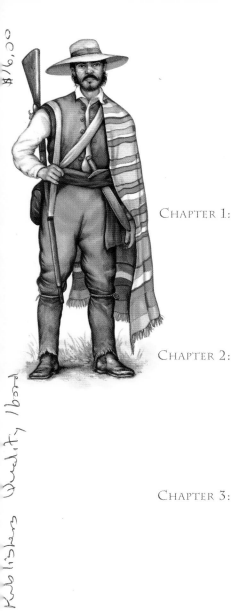

American Battlefields
THE ALAMO
CONTENTS

THE SPANISH IN THE NEW WORLD

T HE MEXICAN CANNONS WERE FINALLY SILENT. For the first time in nearly two weeks, the fighters hunched behind the walls of the fort were able to sleep through the night. They needed the rest, for their fiercest fight was just a few hours away.

The legendary confrontation at the Alamo, a fortified compound in San Antonio, Texas, took place in the predawn hours of March 6, 1836. The battle, which pitted Mexican troops against a small band of Texas colonists, was the turning point in a story that had begun more than three centuries earlier.

In 1521 Spanish adventurer Hernando Cortés and his army defeated the Aztec people, rulers of the region that later became Mexico, at their capital city of Tenochtitlán (modern-day Mexico City). This defeat shattered the Aztecs' grip on the Native American peoples who made up their sprawling empire. Over the next three centuries, Spanish settlers poured into the New World (South, Central, and North America), establishing their power base in Mexico City.

Resources taken from the Americas, including gold, silver, precious stones, and spices, helped make Spain a rich and powerful empire. To keep the flow of wealth coming (and to keep rival nations away), the government needed to extend the empire's borders and increase settlement on the edges of its territory, much as Britain and France were doing farther north.

Hernando Cortés conquered Mexico and claimed its riches for the king of Spain.

One of the most challenging areas lay to the north of Mexico, in sparsely populated Texas. Native American peoples—including Apaches and Comanches—defended their lands there aggressively. Despite the good farming and grazing land in Texas, most Spanish colonists were not interested in risking their lives to put down roots there.

In the early 1700s, the Spanish government grew increasingly concerned about the French, whose ambitions in North America were also growing. Fearing their European rivals would claim Texas for themselves, Spanish leaders ordered the building of five missions, or religious complexes, near present-day San Antonio. One of these missions was the Alamo, originally named San Antonio de Valero.

Using the missions as a base, the Spanish planned to convert native peoples to Christianity. They would "civilize" the natives using education and, if necessary, force. Spanish leaders told settlers that they could find fertile land in Texas (which was true) and that they would be safe (which was not). Clashes between settlers and native peoples continued, and the missions were eventually abandoned.

Before Europeans arrived in Texas, the area was home to Apaches and other Native Americans. Hoping to subdue the native peoples, the Spanish established five missions around San Antonio.

In the late 1770s, when this map was made, San Antonio was just a small military outpost, including a presidio (fort), officers' homes, and the San Antonio de Valero mission—the Alamo.

ORIGINS OF THE ALAMO

One of five missions constructed by the Spanish government around present-day San Antonio, San Antonio de Valero was finished in 1718. For many decades, it served as a religious school for Native American children. The mission was closed in 1793 and thereafter served as an occasional barracks for soldiers from a fort far to the south, in Coahuila, Mexico. From that fort—Alamo del Parras—the dilapidated mission got its new nickname: the Alamo.

THE STRUGGLE FOR FREEDOM

After the United States won its independence from Great Britain at the end of the eighteenth century, it looked hungrily at lands to the west. Many Americans felt it was inevitable that their new nation would one day stretch all the way to the Pacific Ocean—a concept later known as Manifest Destiny. But at the time, Spain and France controlled most of the territory between the Mississippi River and the Pacific. In 1803 the United States bought the province of Louisiana from France (in a deal called the Louisiana Purchase), extending U.S. territory from the Mississippi River to the Rocky Mountains. Soon pioneers began moving into the newly acquired land, much of which bordered Spanish territories in the Southwest.

Anglo-Americans were eager to settle in Texas, but they faced unfair treatment from the Mexican government.

With so many adventurers heading west, Spain renewed its efforts to colonize Texas, which was still a very dangerous and inhospitable place. In 1820 Virginian Moses Austin, the founder of the American lead industry, and his son, Stephen, a lawyer, asked the Spanish government if they could establish a colony in Texas.

While they waited for an answer, a struggle raged in Mexico. Mexican colonists and natives were fighting for independence from Spain. They overthrew Spanish rule in 1821, and the Republic of Mexico was born. The new Mexican government approved the Austins' request. By the end of 1821, Stephen (whose father had died by then) selected a tract of land between the Colorado and Brazos Rivers—deep in Mexican territory—for his colony. He named it San Felipe de Austin.

Austin's colony consisted mainly of farmers and tradesmen, most looking for cheap land and a new start. They were Anglo-Americans—white, English-speaking people from across the border in the United States, mostly of European descent. Despite significant hardships, Austin's colony flourished.

"Every man in Texas is called upon to take up arms in [defense] of his country and his rights."[1]
—Stephen F. Austin

Wary of this increasingly powerful Anglo population, the Mexican government closed its borders to more emigration from the United States, specifically Anglos entering Texas. Mexico gave the Anglo colonists less and less say in how they were taxed and governed. In 1834 Stephen Austin traveled to Mexico City to discuss the matter with General Antonio López de Santa Anna, elected president of Mexico two years earlier.

But Santa Anna had Austin arrested for treason and jailed for a year and a half. Instead of returning to Texas a defeated man, however, Stephen Austin went home convinced that the time had come to take up arms against the Mexican government. He sent horseback riders throughout Texas with posters calling for Texans to fight for their independence.

General Santa Anna was determined not to let Mexico lose control of Texas.

"Freemen of Texas. To Arms!!! To Arms!!! Now's the day, and Now's the hour."[2]
—Poster circulated throughout the Texas colonies.

This 1875 painting shows Stephen Austin formally establishing his colony in Texas.

THE FIRST TEXAN

Without Stephen F. Austin (1793–1836) to spark it, the Texan independence movement might never have gotten off the ground. He was the most respected, admired, and level-headed leader in the region. Trained as a lawyer, he was foremost a skilled negotiator and peacemaker whose goal was to create a thriving colony. While most other influential Texans of the time were trying to make a lot of money, Austin's aim was much more noble and visionary, and others were anxious to follow him.

THE FIRST BATTLE OF THE ALAMO

The defiance of Austin's colonists did not sit well with Santa Anna. In September 1835 he dispatched General Martín Perfecto de Cós, his brother-in-law, with 1,200 men and twenty-one cannons to teach the treasonous Texans a lesson. Once in Texas, General Cós sent a group of men to take back an old cannon, given to colonists to defend the town of Gonzalez against Native Americans. Instead of giving up the cannon, the colonists used it to fire on Cós's men. The war for Texan independence had begun.

News of the confrontation spread quickly. Four hundred Texans grabbed what supplies and ammunition they could find and made camp a few miles from San Antonio de Bexar (present-day San Antonio). Colonel Benjamin Milam led 240 Texans into San Antonio and, after four days of bloody house-to-house fighting, trapped General Cós and his men behind the walls of the Alamo. Cós surrendered, agreeing to leave his weapons and ammunition behind and swearing he would never return.

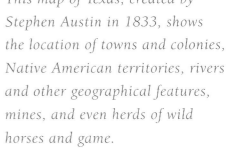

This map of Texas, created by Stephen Austin in 1833, shows the location of towns and colonies, Native American territories, rivers and other geographical features, mines, and even herds of wild horses and game.

> *"Boys! Who will go with me old Ben Milam into Bexar?"[3]*
> —Colonel Ben Milam

Colonel Ben Milam won victory at the first Battle of the Alamo in 1835.

When Santa Anna heard the news, he became enraged. He hastily outfitted and trained a new army for the purpose of crushing the revolt. During this time, the Texans formed a provisional government, led by a businessman named Henry Smith. A colonist named Sam Houston, a former governor of Tennessee, was made head of the army.

Houston knew Santa Anna's first stop would be the Alamo. He sent Colonel Jim Bowie, a famed adventurer, to the mission. Bowie's orders were to blow up the Alamo, so the Mexicans could not use it themselves, and to bring its defenders back to join the army's main force. But when Bowie arrived at the mission, he decided to defy Houston's orders and take a stand. Bowie probably believed his fame would draw hundreds of American soldiers to the fort, where they could beat Santa Anna.

Santa Anna left Mexico City on January 26, 1836, with about 4,000 men. The journey took the Mexican army through difficult terrain and a freak winter snowstorm. The troops ran short of food and water, and more than 500 either died or deserted during the march, which lasted twenty-nine days.

BOWIE'S REAL ESTATE DEAL

Jim Bowie (1799–1836) was the ultimate frontier opportunist— a man with a fearsome fighting reputation, a knack for working the system, and an excellent head for business. He was about to close a deal that would have given him control of more than a million acres in Texas when the trouble started in 1835. Historians have suggested that Bowie decided to stand and fight at the Alamo to protect his interests in Texas real estate.

Sam Houston headed the Texan army.

COMMANDERS IN CONFLICT

SANTA ANNA'S STRATEGY at the Alamo was to encircle the mission, begin a steady bombardment, then attack from all sides simultaneously, until one of the walls could be overwhelmed. Martín Perfecto de Cós, the general who had surrendered the Alamo to the Texans, hoped to be the first to breach the Alamo walls. His reputation had been tarnished in 1835, and he wanted the honor of recapturing the Alamo.

Santa Anna's second in command was Italian-born general Vicente Filisola. Among Santa Anna's other commanders at the Alamo were Cuban-born Manuel Fernandez Castrillón and Antonio Gaona and French-born Adrian Woll. Mexican by birth were generals Jose Vicente Miñon and Joaquín Ramírez y Sesma. Incredibly vain and suspicious, Santa Anna never trusted or respected his officers, and the group he brought to the Alamo was no exception.

"I tell you, the Alamo must fall, and my orders must be obeyed at all hazards."[4]
—Antonio López de Santa Anna

Troops heading north from Mexico City would clash with Americans at the Alamo as well as at Goliad, Gonzalez, and San Jacinto.

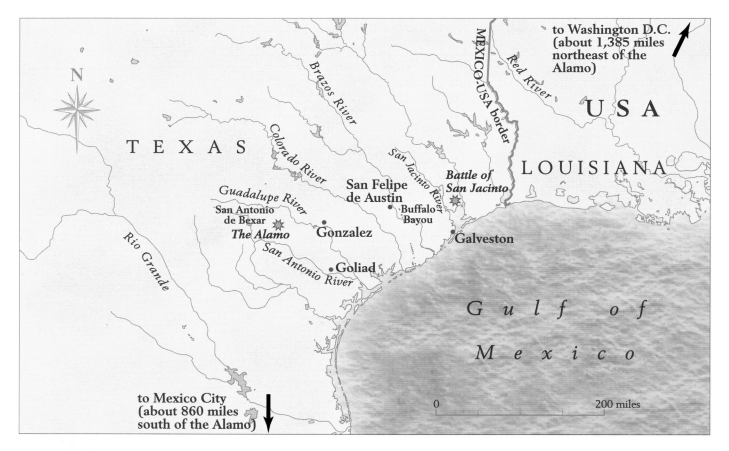

As for the Texan army, it was not an army in the traditional sense. There were no uniforms and no standard-issue weapons or ammunition. The chain of command (established lines of authority) was loose, to say the least. Jim Bowie's decision to defy Houston's direct orders concerning the Alamo is a prime example. Instead of blowing up the mission, Bowie told the officer in charge, Colonel James Neill, to shore up the Alamo's weak defenses and prepare to fight.

The only officer with formal military training anywhere near the Alamo was a colonel named James Fannin. From Fort Defiance in Goliad, about 100 miles away, he and 420 men were preparing to face a Mexican force led by General José Urrea. The boldest of the Texan officers was young William Travis, who arrived at the Alamo seventeen days after Bowie, on February 3, with a contingent of cavalry (soldiers on horseback). Organized and passionate, Travis was the person most qualified to oversee the mission's defense, and he could have taken full authority. But he recognized how much the men looked up to Jim Bowie and decided to share command with him.

Jim Bowie disobeyed orders when he refused to blow up the mission.

SANTA ANNA

Antonio López de Santa Anna (1794–1876), the son of a penniless Spanish immigrant and a Mexican mother, joined the army and developed a taste for pageantry, including fancy uniforms and elaborate ceremonies. Known as a smart military man, he also had a reputation for merciless brutality toward the enemy, his own soldiers, and anyone who stood between him and his ambitions.

RELUCTANT SOLDIERS

The vast majority of soldiers fighting for Santa Anna were doing so against their will. The men "recruited" for the Texas campaign had not volunteered for duty. In fact, many had been snatched at gunpoint from their homes in the Mexican countryside.

Many were poor Native American farmers and laborers, the lowest rung on Mexico's complex social ladder. Their numbers included several hundred Mayans, descendants of an ancient culture from the Yucatán Peninsula.

The men they would face at the Alamo did not have a single day of formal military training between them. Most of the Texans had tangled with hostile Native Americans at one time or another, but defending against an organized military assault was something quite new to them. So, too, was the idea of military conduct, such as following orders, respecting the chain of command, and most of all staying sober. In short, the Alamo defenders were little more than a disorganized rabble. Most were taking a stand to protect their farms, ranches, and families, and their future in Texas. They had built a life in Texas, and many stood to gain great wealth and power if Mexico could be kicked out.

A Texan defender of the Alamo.

A Mexican soldier in uniform.

A PRISONER OF HIS OWN LEGEND

Once Davy Crockett walked through the Alamo gate, he had no choice but to stay. He was one of North America's greatest living heroes—a man who had never backed down in the face of overwhelming odds, whether fighting Native Americans or the president of the United States (as a congressman, Crockett had openly opposed the policies of President Andrew Jackson, knowing that to do so would ruin him). To flee in the face of the Mexican attack would have taken from Crockett his last thing of value: his good name.

Not all of the Alamo defenders had already put down roots in Texas, however. Certainly not Davy Crockett. The legendary frontiersman and former U.S. congressman arrived with a group of volunteers from Tennessee on February 8. They had come seeking their fortunes. They knew that if Texas broke free of Mexico, they stood to become significant landowners. Two nights later, at a dance held in Crockett's honor, a messenger arrived with a note confirming that Santa Anna's army was headed for the Alamo—with thousands of men. As Jim Bowie, Davy Crockett, and William Travis read the note, the gravity of their situation finally became clear.

Davy Crockett was famed as a frontiersman. After the Alamo, his legend would grow even greater.

William Travis, one of the most capable American officers, eventually took charge of the Alamo

"I hope you will do the best you can and I will do the same. Do not be uneasy about me. I am with my friends. Your affectionate father. Farewell."[5]
—Davy Crockett, in a letter written to his children before he rode for the Alamo

OUTMANNED AND OUTGUNNED

The Americans at the Alamo had eighteen cannons, shooting cannonballs ranging in size from six to eighteen pounds. The largest, the eighteen-pounder, was the biggest cannon in all of Texas. The Mexican cannons also varied in size and range, with nine-pounders doing most of the work. In the days following their arrival, Santa Anna's officers began surveying the battlefield to locate the best gun emplacements.

Stephen Austin's personal weapons: two pistols and a tomahawk.

As far as individual weapons were concerned, the overall quality of the firearms at the Alamo was quite poor. A blacksmith traveling in Texas in the 1830s joked that most of the guns he was hired to fix were so bad that he wouldn't have bothered to pick them up from the road. But most of the American fighters were excellent shots, thanks to years of experience hunting animals.

Travis and Bowie, knowing that the heaviest fighting would take place at close range, encouraged their men to use shotguns and short rifles called yagers, which could be loaded and fired quickly. Several men toted Kentucky long rifles, which were accurate to roughly 150 yards. One of Santa Anna's officers recalled years later that an Alamo defender with long, flowing hair and buckskins picked off several Mexican soldiers from a considerable distance with this weapon.

BOWIE KNIVES UP CLOSE

Many American fighters at the Alamo carried Bowie knives, named for Colonel Jim Bowie, who had made the knife famous. This weapon was a long, curved hunting knife that was excellent for throwing and wide enough to gut whatever its user took a swipe at. In other words, it was a hunting knife that worked well on people. Bowie had first used this kind of knife—a gift from his brother—during a fight near Natchez, Mississippi, in 1827.

Mexican troops used British Brown Bess muskets, some of them more than twenty-five years old. These guns were slow to load and sometimes didn't fire correctly. Few, if any, soldiers could fire them with accuracy. So Mexican officers often grouped their troops together to achieve a shotgun effect—firing many bullets at once to better the chance of hitting something.

The Mexicans had bayonets attached to their guns. These would come into play during hand-to-hand combat. The Alamo defenders did not have bayonets, so they had to fight off the bayonet thrusts with their hunting knives and swords. Mexican cavalrymen carried swords such as sabers and long spears called lances. They were Santa Anna's best-trained men, and they used these weapons with deadly efficiency.

> *"All the efforts of the brigade chiefs to instruct the recruits and train them in firing were useless."*[6]
> —José Enrique de la Peña, a Mexican officer

At first, the Mexicans instituted a siege. They fired on the Alamo defenders but did not try to overrun the complex walls.

UNDER SIEGE

The situation General Santa Anna encountered at the Alamo called for a classic siege: surround the enemy, cut off escape and resupply routes, set up a line of guns, and blast away at the defensive walls. Santa Anna knew that the defenders, outnumbered about ten to one, had nowhere to go and would eventually run low on food, ammunition, and other supplies. The Mexican forces planned to fire at the Texans until their defenses collapsed or their morale became so low that they simply surrendered. In the end, Santa Anna changed his strategy and ordered an attack.

A BIRD'S-EYE VIEW

The Alamo was a walled compound, measuring 440 yards around the perimeter, or outside. Made of heavy stone as well as mud bricks, the walls were quite thick in most places, offering good protection against bombardment. But there were weak spots and even some breaks in the walls. In those areas, the defenders built makeshift barricades. The height of the walls varied.

Since the Alamo had been constructed as a mission, not a fort, it didn't have built-in spots from which the defenders could fire weapons. So the Texans built earthen ramps and ledges that allowed them to fire over the mission walls at oncoming troops. But to take their shots, the Texans had to stand up on the ledges, thereby exposing themselves to enemy fire.

> "Ignorant of the art of war, incapable of discipline, and renowned for insubordination."[7]
> —Evaluation of Anglo soldiers by José María Tornel, Mexican Minister of War

The defenders turned many of the old mission buildings into barracks and headquarters.

Mexican assault on the Alamo

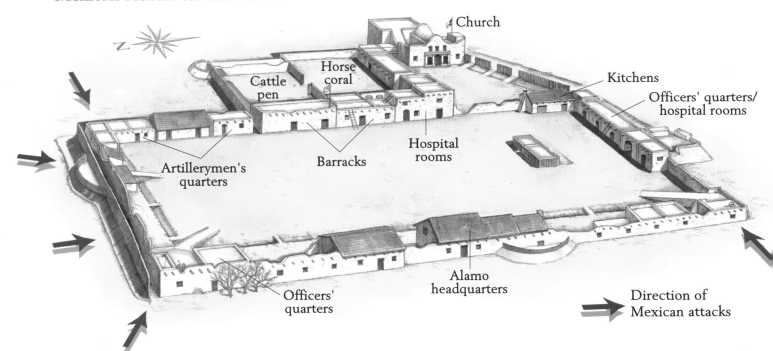

Church

Horse coral

Cattle pen

Kitchens

Officers' quarters/ hospital rooms

Artillerymen's quarters

Barracks

Hospital rooms

Officers' quarters

Alamo headquarters

Direction of Mexican attacks

ALAMO FAMILIES

Not everyone behind the walls of the Alamo was a fighter. Some were family members of soldiers. Others were townspeople who had come to the fort seeking protection from oncoming Mexican troops. Although many civilians left the Alamo just before the attack, others remained, including several women and children. Juana Alsbury, Jim Bowie's sister-in-law, lived through the fighting along with her younger sister, Gertrudis. So did Susannah Dickinson, the teenage bride of Captain Almeron Dickinson, and their baby daughter.

Susannah Dickinson was one of several women trapped inside the Alamo.

Estimates of the number of fighters involved in the battle have fluctuated wildly over the years. Even with experienced historians poring over the records, it has been difficult to come up with accurate figures. The best estimates place the number of Texans between 182 and 250 and the number of Mexicans at slightly less than 2,000. (In the past, that figure was put as high as 7,000, by people trying to boost the heroism of the defenders.)

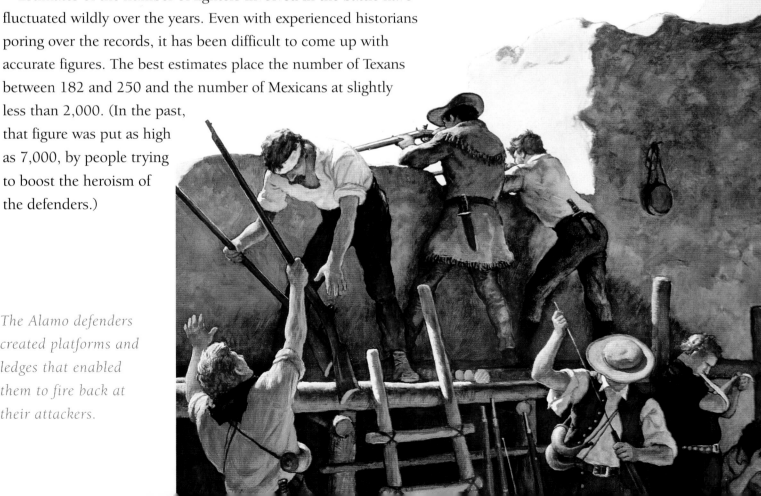

The Alamo defenders created platforms and ledges that enabled them to fire back at their attackers.

THE BATTLE BEGINS

The Mexican army arrived in San Antonio on February 23. Its first act was to raise a red flag above San Fernando Cathedral in the town of San Antonio—a message to the rebels that they could expect no mercy. The response from the Alamo was a defiant cannon blast.

The next day, the Mexicans began a barrage with artillery (cannons). The shelling would continue, with few breaks, for the next twelve days. Between cannon blasts, the Mexicans played musical instruments and traded insults and obscenities with the Alamo defenders.

When evening fell on the first day of shelling, everyone in the mission was amazed to find that no one had been killed, and none of their cannons had been badly damaged. By this time, William Travis had assumed full

"These men were defiant to the last. From the windows and parapets of the low buildings, when taunted by Mexican troops, they shouted back their defiance in the liveliest terms."[8]
—A Mexican soldier writing about the Alamo defenders

A map drawn by one of Santa Anna's soldiers at the time of the battle.

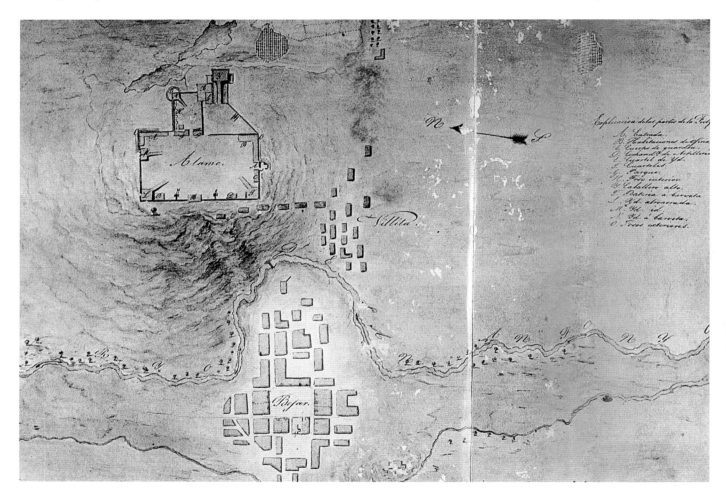

command of the Alamo defenses. Jim Bowie, suffering from the effects of an old bout with cholera, was too weak to stand.

Travis sent a messenger galloping through enemy lines with a letter for Sam Houston, who was gathering his remaining forces near San Felipe de Austin and trying to figure out where Santa Anna's army would go next. Travis reported that the Texans' flag was still flying proudly, but that he needed reinforcements.

VICTORY OR DEATH!

Twenty-six-year-old William Travis wanted to leave his mark on the world. His desperate letter to Sam Houston did just that. Addressed to the "People of Texas & all Americans in the world," it painted a glorious picture of the first day's fighting but also revealed the hopelessness of the defenders' situation.

Travis pleaded for help, but he ended the letter with a promise to die like a soldier if help did not reach the Alamo in time. He signed it with the famous words "Victory or Death."

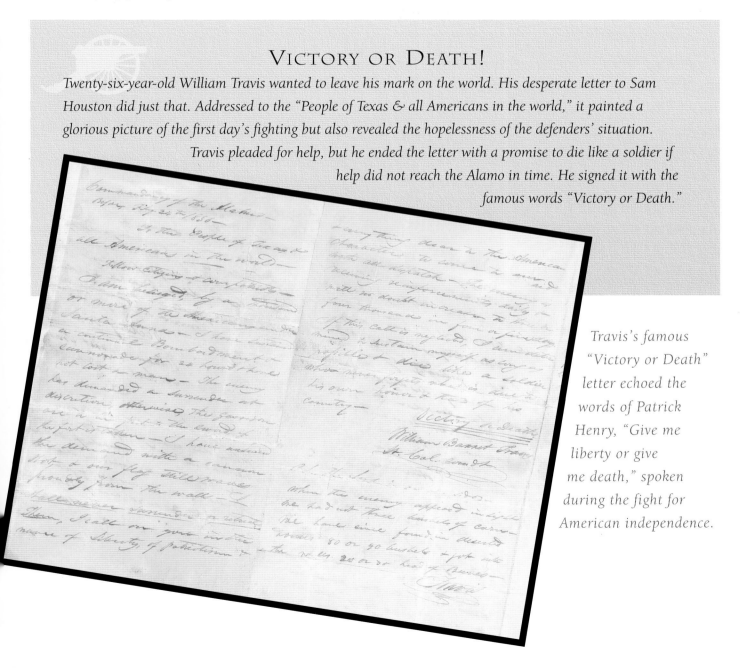

Travis's famous "Victory or Death" letter echoed the words of Patrick Henry, "Give me liberty or give me death," spoken during the fight for American independence.

HELP ARRIVES

When the sun came up on the first day of March, the Alamo defenders had survived almost a week of constant shelling without a single death. A sentry was startled to see a group of thirty-two horses galloping toward the main gate just after sunrise. He squeezed off a shot, hitting one rider in the foot before realizing his mistake. These were not Mexican cavalry but Texan reinforcements from Gonzalez. They had broken through Santa Anna's lines.

Their arrival lifted the spirits of the defenders. Davy Crockett serenaded them on his fiddle, accompanied by a fellow named John McGregor on bagpipes. Almost immediately, Travis's bedraggled men began to speculate about Colonel James Fannin and his 420 soldiers at Fort Defiance in Goliad. Surely, the men thought, these Gonzalez riders were just the trickle before the flood came from Goliad.

Travis anxiously awaited the return of James Bonham, who had been riding back and forth between the Alamo and Fort

FANNIN'S FOLLY

James Fannin decided not to send reinforcements to the Alamo for fear that his own garrison would soon be overwhelmed. When General José Urrea's Mexican forces neared, Fannin and his men left the fort and made a run for it. Urrea's soldiers later rounded them up and executed them on March 27.

James Bonham served as a messenger during the siege, seeking help from Fort Defiance.

Defiance. Bonham got back to the Alamo on March 3 with grim news: no help would be coming. Fannin had decided to stay put. The Alamo, with probably fewer than 200 able-bodied men, was on its own.

By March 5 Santa Anna had grown tired of his siege and gathered his officers to plan an all-out attack. He ordered them to storm the mission just before sunrise the next day. He would gamble all of his troops in a single, overwhelming assault.

Santa Anna finally gave the order to storm the Alamo walls.

"Texas expects every man to do his duty."[9]
—Provisional Governor Henry Smith

MASSACRE

At 5:30 in the morning on March 6, four columns of 400 to 500 men each began moving toward the Alamo's four walls. At daybreak, cries of "Viva Santa Anna" ("Hurrah for Santa Anna") suddenly filled the air, waking the defenders from their slumber. Each defender had several guns loaded and ready, and in the opening minutes of the battle, the advancing troops were cut to ribbons by a thousand shots. The Alamo cannons, stuffed with scrap metal and chains, took down several hundred attackers.

This dramatic painting, created in 1905, shows chaotic fighting inside the Alamo.

Despite these initial volleys, the Mexicans soon reached the walls of the Alamo. As the Texans rose above the walls to fire down on their enemy, they were greeted with hails of lead. William Travis was among the first to go, taking a bullet to the forehead.

The first breakthrough came at the north wall. The Texans fell back and continued to fire away. Next, the southwest corner gave way. A group of fifty or more Americans made a break for the road to Gonzalez but were quickly wiped out by Mexican cavalry. The others retreated to a barracks building inside the fort. They slammed the thick door, reinforced with wooden braces and a crossbar, and continued to fire from the barracks' windows. The Mexicans turned the Alamo's cannons around and blew the door off its hinges, then

DID THE TEXANS HAVE A CHANCE?

Historians still argue whether so few Texans had any chance against the large Mexican force. With reinforcements, they might have held out longer or even repelled the attack. But the defense was an exceedingly complicated one, requiring skill and experience that William Travis and the other officers simply did not have.

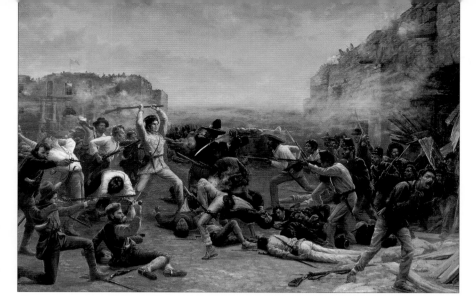

This 1903 painting shows a defiant Davy Crockett holding his ground against Mexican attackers.

> "I do not want to see those men living. Shoot them."[10]
> —Santa Anna's orders regarding Crockett and his fellow survivors

cleared the barracks in savage, hand-to-hand fighting. They swept through a room that served as a makeshift hospital, finishing off the sick and wounded. Jim Bowie, unable to rise from his cot, was killed where he lay.

Though the fighting lasted less than thirty minutes, the violence went on for almost an hour. Mexican soldiers continued to stab and shoot the Alamo defenders long after they were dead. More than 500 Mexicans also lay dead or dying. In the end, none of the Alamo defenders survived. Santa Anna ordered their bodies to be burned.

But it wasn't a total massacre. The women and children in the fort, along with William Travis's slave, Joe, were allowed to leave unharmed. Most walked toward the nearest town, Gonzalez.

Historians believe that Crockett and others were captured and then executed.

HOW DID DAVY DIE?

According to a diary account dictated years later by Mexican officer José Enrique de la Peña, Davy Crockett and five other Tennessee fighters were captured alive after they ran out of ammunition in the Alamo chapel. Santa Anna, enraged by his appalling losses, had Crockett and the others put to the sword. Scientists and historians have examined the de la Peña diaries—discovered in an attic in 1954—and believe them to be authentic.

SHOWDOWN AT SAN JACINTO

O N MARCH 2, 1836—four days before Santa Anna's final assault on the Alamo—Texas declared its independence from Mexico. Although Texans may have been free on paper, in reality they were facing an army seeking to restore Mexican control in Texas. Sam Houston made his way to Gonzalez, where scouts informed him that Alamo widow Susannah Dickinson had just walked into town with her infant daughter. Her story of the carnage spread quickly throughout Texas. Colonists packed up their belongings and fled by the thousands.

Santa Anna, meanwhile, pursued the main force of the Texas army, commanded by Houston. On April 19 the Texans moved across the Buffalo Bayou and prepared to engage Santa Anna, whose men were working day and night to fortify their position. On the afternoon of April 21, the Mexicans—certain there would be no evening attack—decided it was safe to relax. Many, including Santa Anna, repaired to their tents for a nap.

Above: Texas's declaration of independence.

The Texans fought with ferocity at San Jacinto. Mexican casualties were extensive there.

At 4:30 p.m., two cannonballs came screaming into Santa Anna's camp. Houston's modest force, numbering less than 1,000 men, came pouring over the small hill that stood between the two armies. Caught by surprise, the Mexicans were unable to offer resistance. The Texans—yelling "Remember Goliad!" and "Remember the Alamo!"—went on a rampage. The Battle of San Jacinto, as the encounter was called, was over in a matter of minutes. While some Mexicans fled, more than 600 were killed, while only nine Texans lost their lives.

> *"This morning we are in preparation to meet Santa Anna. It is the only chance of saving Texas. We go to conquer."*[11]
> —Sam Houston

SAM HOUSTON

Sam Houston (1793–1863) would become one of America's most enduring nineteenth-century heroes. The morning of the Battle of San Jacinto, however, found him at odds with his men. Houston's officers thought that by allowing Santa Anna to fortify his position the night before, they had lost a golden opportunity. As it turned out, Houston's attack that afternoon came at exactly the right time. (The modern-day city of Houston, named after the famous commander, covers the area where the battle took place.)

A captured Santa Anna is brought to Sam Houston. Houston reclines because his foot is wounded.

25

INDEPENDENCE!

In the days that followed the Battle of San Jacinto, many of the soldiers who had fled the Mexican camp were rounded up. These included General Santa Anna, who had hidden in a marsh wearing an enlisted man's uniform. (His own troops gave him away, shouting "El Presidente" as he passed them.) Houston's men begged him to hang Santa Anna. Instead, Houston persuaded the general to instruct the remnants of his army to leave Texas.

> *"I am general Antonio López de Santa Anna, President of Mexico, commander-in-chief of the army of operations, and I put myself at the disposition of the brave general Houston. I wish to be treated as a general should be when a prisoner of war."[12]*
> —Santa Anna, upon his capture at San Jacinto

On May 14, 1836, Santa Anna signed the Treaty of Velasco, which guaranteed that Mexico would recognize Texas's independence. That summer, the new Republic of Texas held its first general election. Sam Houston became president. He appointed Stephen Austin as secretary of state.

Texans wanted their new independent nation to join the growing United States of America, partly for protection against Mexico. Although Texas voters approved a proposal to join the United States, they had to wait nearly ten years for statehood. At the time, the slavery debate was raging in the United States. Texas, a slave state, could not join the Union until a free state was admitted to "balance" it. In 1845 Texas finally became part of the United States.

Stephen Austin became secretary of state in the new Republic of Texas. The city of Austin, the Texas capital, is named for him.

MANIFEST DESTINY

During the mid-1840s, American politicians and other leaders began using the term "Manifest Destiny." The term expressed the idea that the United States—because of its growing power and population—was destined to acquire or control all of the territory between the Atlantic and Pacific Oceans. Shortly after the Mexican War (1846–1848), this vision largely became a reality.

One year later, in 1846, war erupted between the United States and Mexico. Santa Anna had long plotted to recapture the land lost through his military blunders. He sent troops across the Rio Grande, the river separating Mexico and Texas, in April 1846. The United States drove the Mexicans out of Texas and launched a full-scale invasion of Mexico, eventually capturing Mexico City.

Mexico was defeated in 1848. The peace treaty following the war required Mexico to sell hundreds of thousands of square miles of land, comprising much of modern-day Arizona, California, Nevada, New Mexico, Wyoming, and Utah. Many historians believe that the battle for the Alamo sparked the chain of events that led to this crucial development in U. S. history.

American forces triumphed in the Mexican War. After the war, the United States acquired vast amounts of territory in the American Southwest.

In the years prior to the Civil War, the Alamo was used as an army supply depot. This photograph was taken sometime in the mid- to late 1800s.

THE ALAMO TODAY

Today the Alamo serves as a shrine, a source of inspiration, and a tourist destination. It has also been the subject of more than a dozen feature films. Tourist shops near the site sell Alamo hats, key chains, T-shirts, snow globes, and every other manner of modern artifact. Indeed, on a visit to San Antonio, it is impossible to walk more than a block or two without seeing someone wearing (or selling) an Alamo souvenir.

But the Alamo presented to tourists bears little resemblance to the Alamo of the great battle. In 1850 the U.S. Army remodeled the complex, destroying or dismantling many of the original buildings. It wasn't until the early 1900s that anyone tried to preserve and restore the buildings, and by then there was little left to preserve—only the chapel and a few sections of barracks remained.

The remaining structures sit right in the heart of the city, surrounded by a tourist complex complete with small parks, gift shops, and museum buildings. The site does not look like a fort, which is a surprise to most visitors. Still, the Alamo is by far the most popular tourist attraction in Texas and is often used as a backdrop for political events.

A monument at Alamo Plaza features statues of James Bonham (left), Jim Bowie (right), and other defenders.

The Alamo lives on in American art and folklore. In 1960 Hollywood produced The Alamo, *directed by and starring John Wayne. Wayne played Davy Crockett.*

Although it doesn't look like the original site, the Alamo remains a place of reverence. People making too much noise are asked to lower their voices. Photography is discouraged inside the chapel, and men are asked to remove their hats when they enter.

In the years since the battle, American stories and songs have painted the Alamo defenders as selfless patriots and the Mexicans as scoundrels. But in recent years, historical research has given us a new, more complex image of the battle. Many defenders came to the Alamo not out of a sense of patriotism, but because of greed, bravado, bad timing, or bad luck. While some were noble fighters, others were lowlifes, scoundrels, and opportunists. And the Mexican attackers, far from being ruthless devils, were largely frightened and inexperienced young men. They were only doing their jobs—trying to maintain Mexican control on Mexican soil.

Still, few places in the United States speak louder to the spirit and fortitude of the American frontiersman than the Alamo. In the sixteen-plus decades since the famous battle, the fort has become a symbol of bravery, sacrifice, freedom, and justice—for Americans, if not for Mexicans.

THE LEGEND OF DAVY CROCKETT

As Davy Crockett contemplated his doom in the days before Santa Anna attacked the Alamo, he could not have begun to imagine how his legend would grow. In the years after his death, the famous fighter was acclaimed in stories, movies, and songs. In the mid-1950s, the "Crockett craze" reached its zenith with a Walt Disney movie and a serialized version of his life on television. Inspired by these shows, thousands of young viewers bought a variety of Davy Crockett toys and costumes, including replicas of his famous coonskin cap.

The chapel at the Alamo as it appears today.

"Remember the Alamo"
—America's most famous battle cry

TIMELINE

1718: The Alamo is constructed in San Antonio de Bexar.

1793: The mission is abandoned and falls into disrepair.

1821: Mexico wins independence from Spain after eleven years of civil war; Moses and Stephen Austin are granted permission to establish a colony in Texas.

1830: The Texas colony grows to a population of more than 20,000.

1834: Stephen Austin travels to Mexico City to fight for rights for Texas colonists. He is arrested and imprisoned there.

1835: *September 9*: Stephen Austin returns to Texas after imprisonment in Mexico City.
October 2: Colonists drive off Mexican forces at Gonzalez.
October 11: Stephen Austin leads a force from Goliad to San Antonio.
November 3: Sam Houston is named commander in chief of the Texan army.
November 24: Stephen Austin leaves San Antonio to get guns, ammunition, and volunteer soldiers from the United States.
December 10: General Cós surrenders his forces at the Alamo.

1836: *January 17*: Sam Houston orders Jim Bowie to destroy the Alamo.
February 3: William Travis arrives at the Alamo.
February 8: Davy Crockett arrives at the Alamo.
February 23: Santa Anna arrives in San Antonio and begins a siege of the Alamo.
March 6: Texans are defeated at the Alamo.
April 21: Mexicans are defeated at the Battle of San Jacinto.

1850: The U.S. Army remodels the Alamo, destroying or dismantling most of the original structures.

1876: The army stops using the Alamo.

1883: The state of Texas purchases the property.

1905: The Daughters of the Republic of Texas take over custody and care of the Alamo.

1914: A silent movie, *The Siege and Fall of the Alamo*, is filmed on location.

1937: The city of San Antonio purchases the last remaining parcel of land around the Alamo.

1939: The Alamo is reproduced at the Texas exhibit at the 1939 World's Fair in New York.

1954: *Davy Crockett, Indian Fighter* airs on television.

1955: *Davy Crockett, King of the Wild Frontier* plays at movie theaters.

1960: John Wayne stars in the hit movie *The Alamo*.

1966: The Alamo is listed on the National Register of Historic Places.

1997: The Wall of History, an exhibit outlining the history of Texas and the Alamo, is dedicated at the Alamo.

GLOSSARY

Anglo-Americans—white, English-speaking North Americans, primarily of European descent

artillery—large guns such as cannons

barrage—intense artillery fire concentrated on a specific target

bayonet—a steel blade attached to the end of a rifle, used for hand-to-hand combat

cavalry—soldiers mounted on horseback

chain of command—lines of authority (who must take orders from whom) used in the military and other organizations

convert—to bring about a change in religious belief

emplacement—a prepared position for a weapon or another piece of military equipment

emigration—the movement of people from their places of residence for the purpose of establishing permanent homes elsewhere

Manifest Destiny—the idea, popular in the mid-1800s, that the United States would inevitably control all North American territory between the Atlantic and Pacific Oceans

mission—In Texas and other parts of North America, a religious complex where Spanish leaders tried to convert Native Americans to Catholicism

siege—a military blockade of a city or fort, usually accompanied by a military attack

FURTHER INFORMATION

BOOKS TO READ

Bredeson, Carmen. *Texas*. Tarrytown, NY: Benchmark Books, 1997.

Fears, Ann, ed. *The Autobiography of Santa Anna*. Austin, TX: State House Press, 1988.

Fritz, Jean. *Make Way for Sam Houston*. Toronto: General Publishing, 1986.

Leone, Bruno. *The Mexican War of Independence*. San Diego: Lucent Books, 1997.

Murphy, Jim. *Inside the Alamo*. New York: Delacorte Press, 2003.

Reton, Walter. *The Story of Davy Crockett, Frontier Hero*. Milwaukee: Gareth Stevens Publishing, 1997.

Riehecky, Janet. *The Siege of the Alamo*. Milwaukee: World Almanac Library, 2002.

PLACES TO VISIT

The Alamo, San Antonio, Texas
http://www.thealamo.org
Austin Colony, Brazoria County Historical Museum, Angleton, Texas
http://www.bchm.org
Goliad, Texas
http://www.tpwd.state.tx.us/expltx/eft/goliad/historic.htm
Gonzalez, Texas
http://www.gonzalestexas.com

WEBSITES

The Alamo
http://www.thealamo.org
Daughters of the Republic of Texas Library
http://www.drtl.org
The American West
http://www.americanwest.com
Lone Star Junction
http://www.lsjunction.com

NOTES

1. Jeff Long, *Duel of Eagles: The Mexican and U.S. Fight for the Alamo* (New York: William Morrow and Company, 1990), 59.
2. Ibid., 60.
3. Ibid., 77.
4. Ibid., 222.
5. Lon Tinke, *Thirteen Days to Glory: The Siege of the Alamo* (College Station, TX: Texas A&M University Press, 1985), 134.
6. Long, *Duel of Eagles*, 142.
7. Edward P. Hoyt, *The Alamo: An Illustrated History* (Dallas: Taylor Trade Publishing, 1999), 167.
8. Long, *Duel of Eagles*, 194.
9. Hoyt, *The Alamo*, 87.
10. Long, *Duel of Eagles*, 259.
11. Ibid., 306.
12. Ibid., 316.

INDEX